Wolf Coloring Book For Adults

Wolf Coloring Book containing various Wolves filled with intricate and stress relieving patterns

Colorong Books For Adults: Vol 8

by The Coloring Book People

ISBN-13: 978-1534909236

ISBN-10: 1534909230

PREVIEW

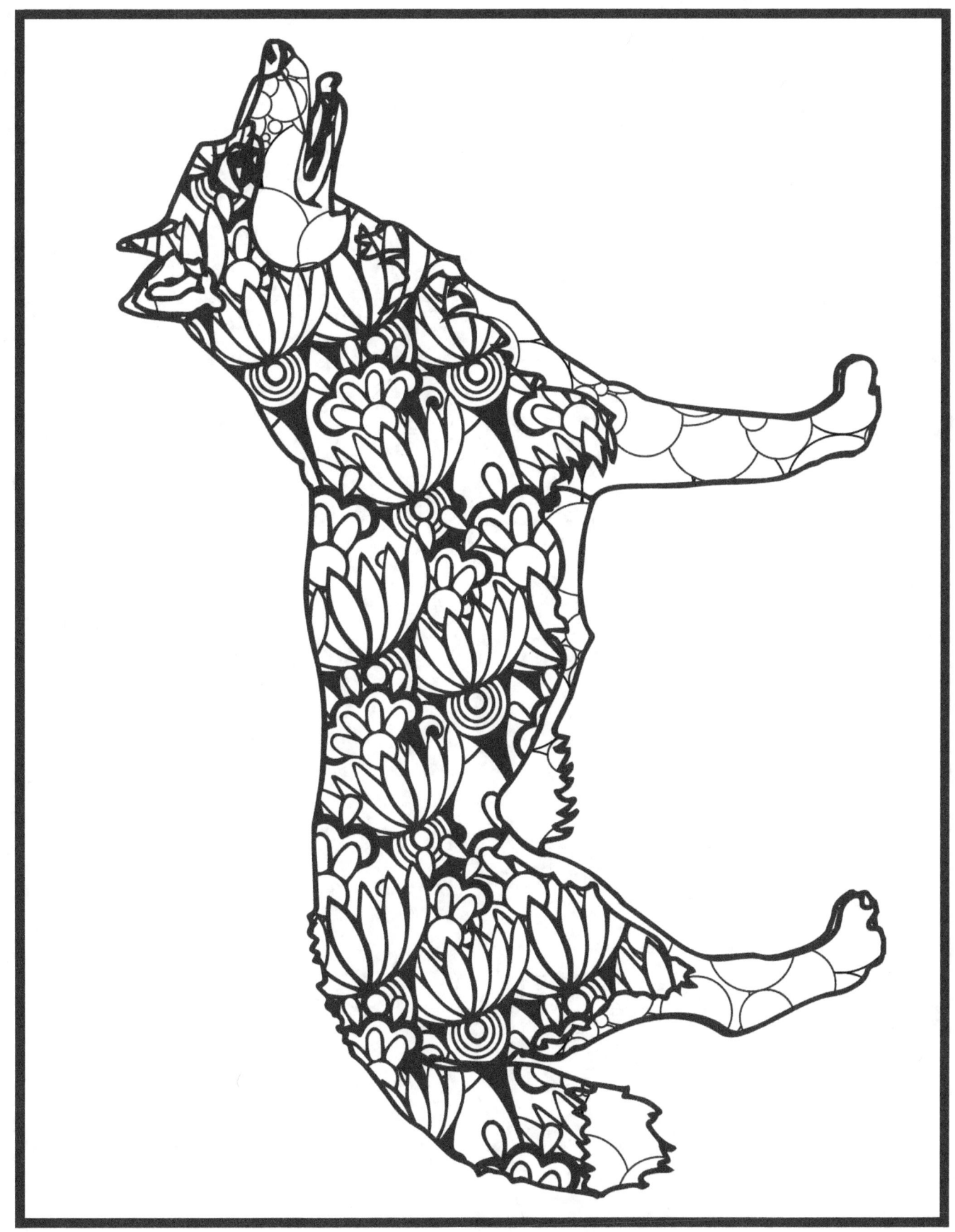

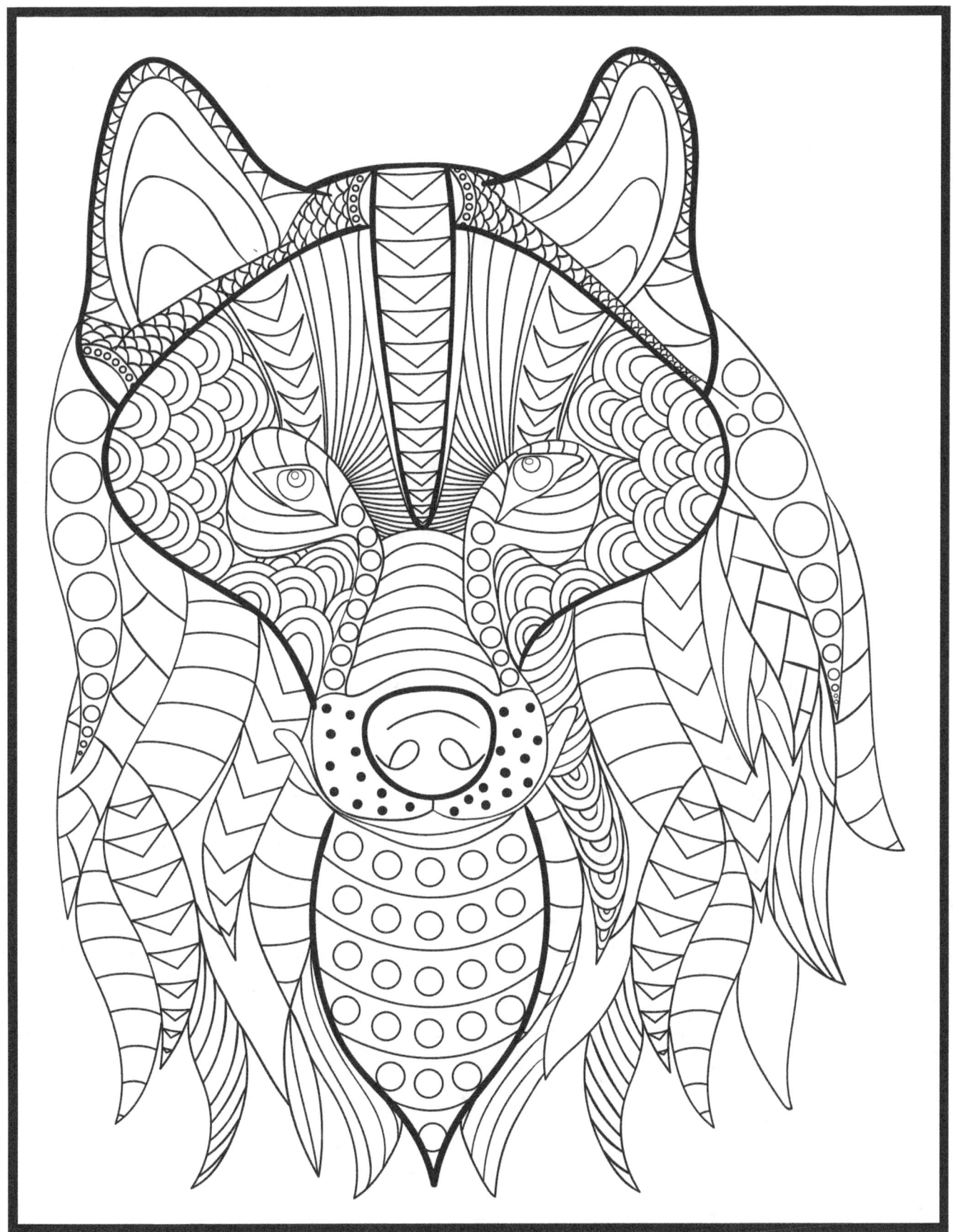

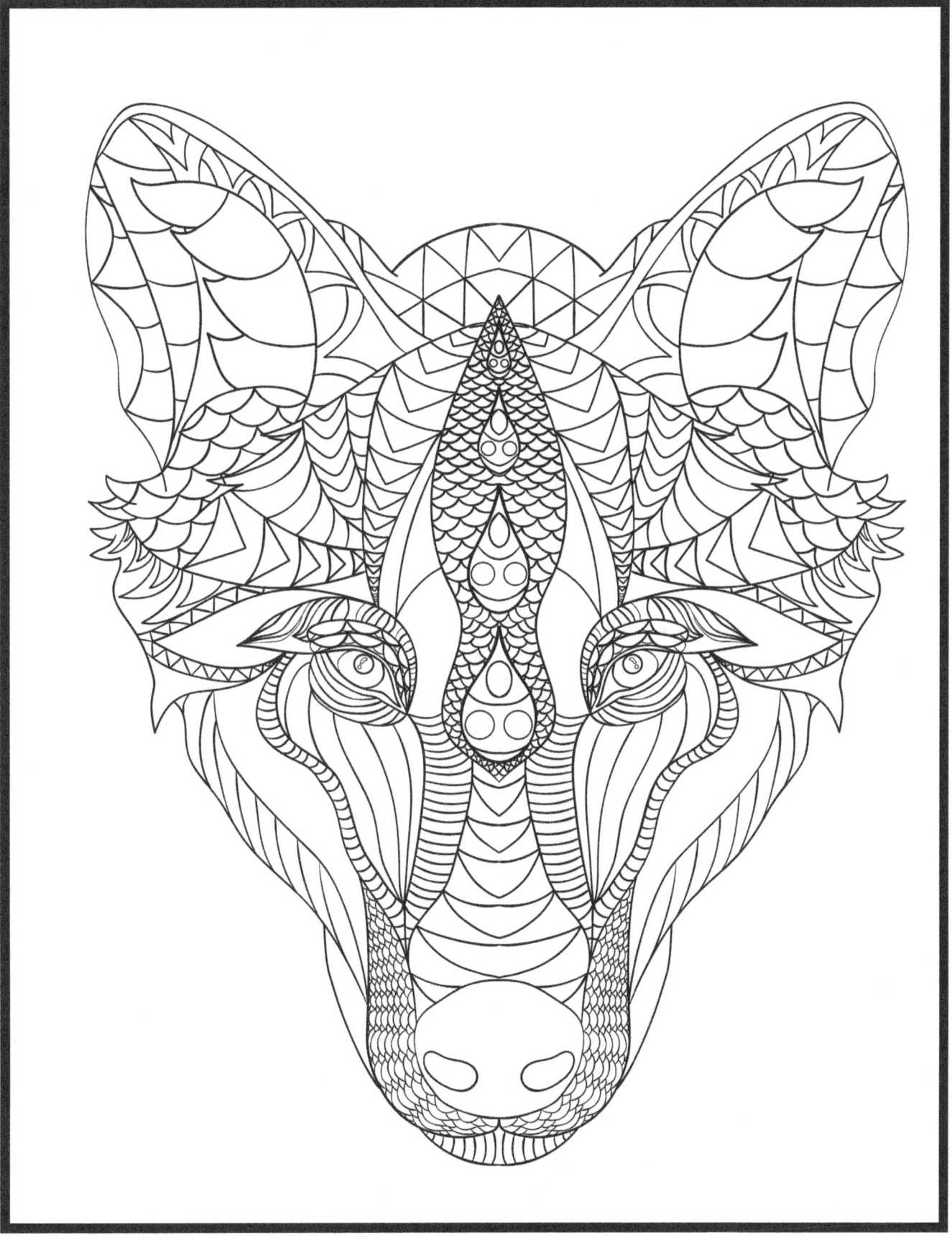

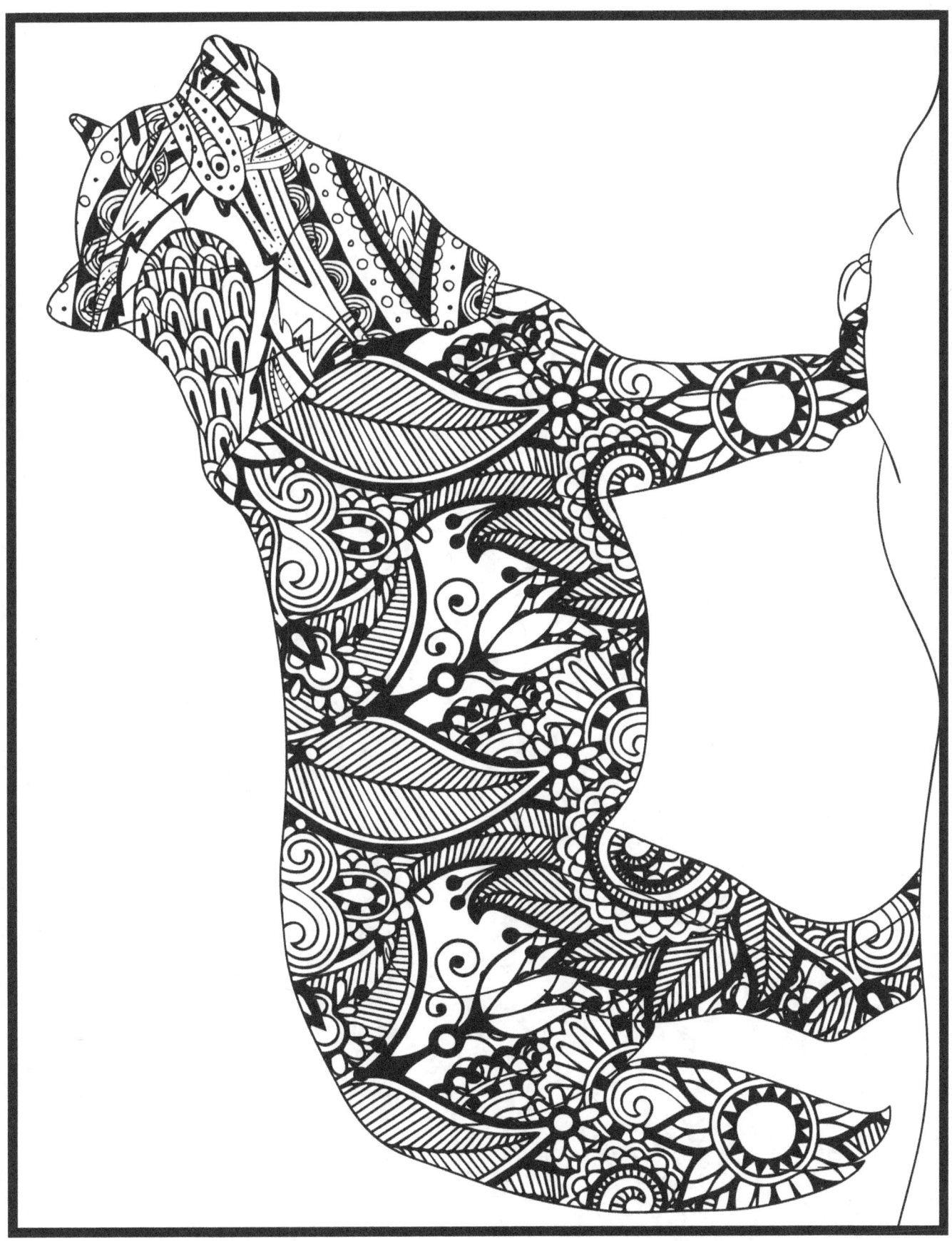

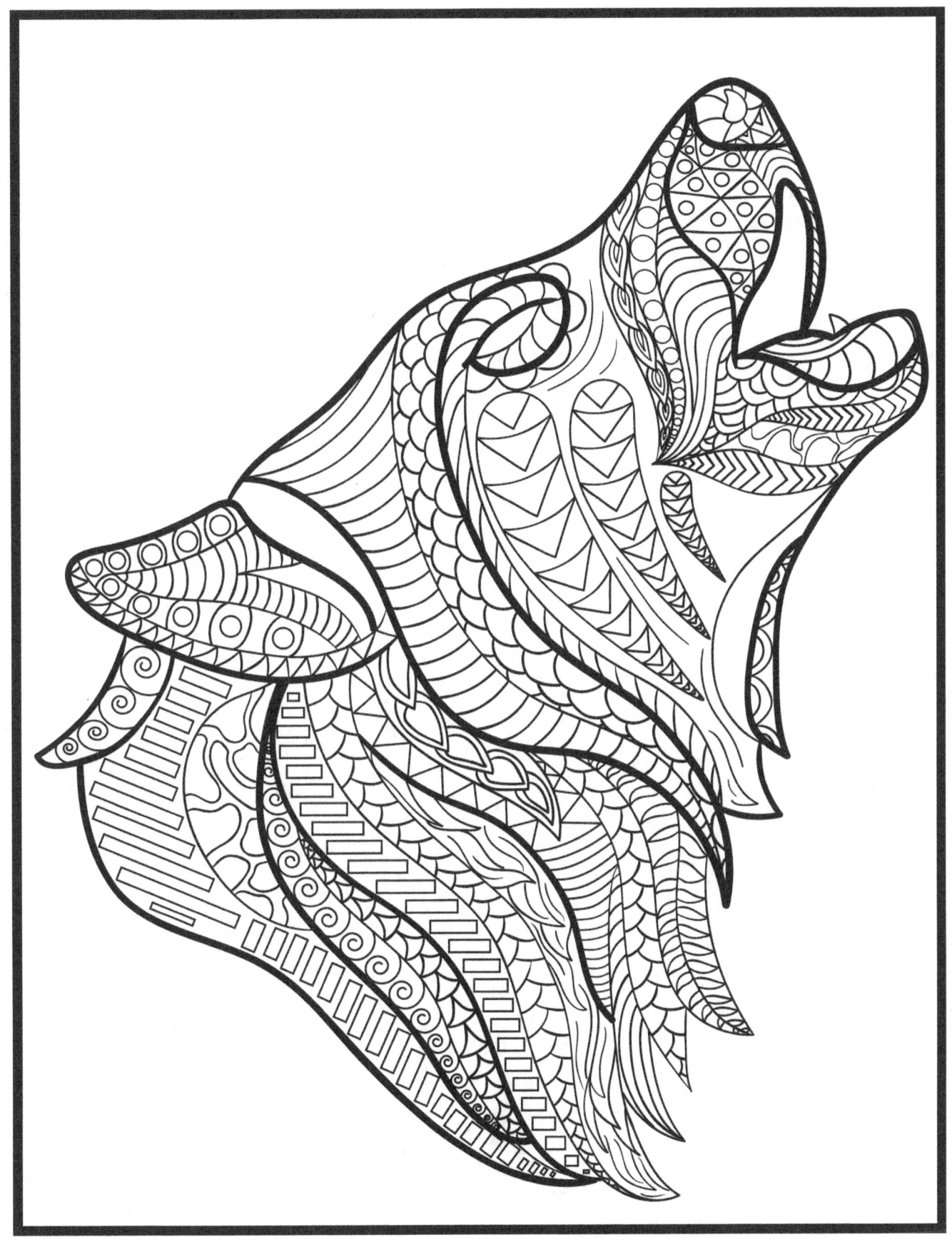

COLOR TEST PAGE

COLOR TEST PAGE